> The ultimate aim of the human mind,
>
> In all its efforts,
>
> Is to become acquainted with truth
>
> ~Eliza Farnham

Contents

Introduction	3
1. Beginnings	8
2. Not Alone	11
3. Details	13
4. A Problem Arises	15
5. Solving the Problem	20
6. Religion vs The Birthing	23
7. The Way	26
8. Creation	28
9. The Stage	34
10. The Fall	38
11. The Awakening	41
12. The Deceiver	43
13. A Tool in the Shed	47
14. The Result of Evil	50
15. New Life & Understanding	56
16. Recap	60
17. The Plan	63
18. Bridging the Gap	72
19. Dispensations	75
20. Conclusion	84
21. About the Author	92

INTRODUCTION

I don't think there has ever been a person that has ever existed, that has not asked the question,

"What is the meaning of life?"

I am convinced that I understand the answer to this question! I am not trying to be arrogant, and I certainly do not know everything, I don't even know a lot of things that make this world tick! You see knowledge of things in this world, and the meaning of life are two completely different things. For example, I may not know the intricate workings of a computer, but I don't know why the computer is there and what it is used for. It is similar with life. No one knows the workings of everything on this planet, or of spiritual matters, but we can know the meaning of life, who we are and why we are here.

I have spent the last 35 plus years seeking to understand the meaning of life. Now, after 3 marriages, and raising a half dozen kids, and being self-employed most of my life along with other things both good and bad that have happened in my life, I believe I have uncovered the answer to this question that seems to elude multitudes of people from all generations and walks of life.

It's not that I have a patent on truth, nor do I believe that I am the only one who has been able to grasp the answers to this question, but I will say that I do believe that I have a unique perspective of this topic, as hopefully you will soon discover.

So please join me on this journey of revelation, this journey that is a combination of both frustration and elation. Frustration from not knowing the answers to certain things about life and the struggle to understand, to elation when something finally clicks in our soul and gives us a deeper look into the mysteries of life and of why we are here.

I hope this book becomes one of mostly elation for its readers and less of frustration. However, it has been my experience that elation is usually preceded by frustration of some sort.
Either way, I believe growth will come as a result of having read this book. At the very least, it will be one more idea you can check off should you decide I'm full of it! I believe however that you will at the very least, view my findings as interesting, and something to seriously ponder.

This book is the accumulation of almost four decades of searching for God. Even more than that, searching for truth. In my opinion you cannot seek the meaning to life and not research the possibility of a divine mastermind. The world is too orderly to have come about from nothing. The very fact that we humans have a concept of a hereafter seemingly built into our psyche, lends to the idea at the very least, that there is a higher power. I personally do not understand atheism. I think it takes more faith to believe that there is no

God, and that everything on this planet, including the planet itself happened out of nothing! The very order of things screams intelligent design!

Did you know that caterpillars, after forming their cocoon around themselves, liquify and renew themselves as butterfly's? Wow! Even nature cries out the existence of a mind and a power that is beyond anything we can imagine! The life of the caterpillar being made new into the butterfly is a testimony from nature of what happens to us under certain circumstances.

Though the inspiration for this book comes from scripture, I decided not to make it clinical in the sense that there is a scriptural reference in every paragraph. That can often get boring, and boring can cause a person to lose interest. However, there are scriptural references in a few places where I decided that it was truly needed to really get the point across. It is written this way to spark interest and give a perspective to the title that I have never read in other books. That does not mean that similar works do not exist.

Scripture is not the only inspiration for this book. A desire to know truth, to know what lies beyond this existence. It just so happens that in finding truth, the scriptures, mostly Paul's writings in the Bible, become a beacon of light that open the door to understanding.

My hope and prayer are that you the reader will enjoy the deep perspectives laid down in this book and that they aid you in your search to understanding the meaning of life for yourself, and in the perspective of your own personality. This is the meaning of life to me.
Scott Halbert

The Meaning of Life

Beginnings

We are born into this world completely helpless. We cannot feed ourselves, cloth ourselves or even use the restroom by ourselves! We are so small and helpless that we need help with everything we do.
We go through life gradually learning the ins and outs of how to do all those things that we couldn't do when we were born, searching for our place in this world.
Then, there comes a time in everyone's life, whether it be in the midst of a crisis, be it health, financial or relational, or just a flippant thought of the future and the hereafter, and we find ourselves pondering this question. "What is the meaning of life? "
What is all of this for? Do we just exist for 70-100 years, some less, some more and then we die? Is this all just a game where the one who gains the most stuff wins?

Maybe we have children, maybe we don't. At least if we have children our bloodline will carry on, but what about our soul? Do we even have one? If we do what does our soul consist of?

What is the point of all this running around and trying to better ourselves, the search for things like honor or morality, if there is nothing beyond this world of getting all we can until we die?

One of the biggest problems we have in the world today in society is getting further and further from what once gave us something to hold on to spiritually.

Life can be exciting for a time when everything is new and we are experiencing different stimuli, like new things, new relationships and new jobs and experiences. Then all the sudden BOOM! Something happens that throws a wrench in all those new and fun experiences. Or, the new and fun experiences were never, new and fun!

No one escapes going through crisis in their life. No one! Some people have several! Sometimes it's adversity in our lives that brings us to the point of questioning. Sometimes it's nearing deaths door, and we wonder what's on the other side.

Life has a way putting the stops on the new and fun and backing us into a corner. Sometimes it's the loss of a job, or a failed marriage. Sometimes substance abuse takes over a life, or the death of a loved one, or news of our own impending premature demise! Sometimes we have everything we will ever need or want, yet we still can't shake that emptiness inside that is inherent in all of us.

These things can sometimes break us and land us in the spot that all humans land at some point in their life. That, "What Is the Meaning of Life," spot! What is the point of all this?

Not Alone

I'm assuming that because you are reading this book, that you are in that spot! Or have been there and though things may be a little better now, in the back of your mind you fear it may return. Am I right? If not, just wait, it will come!
I read an article a few months ago that the richest person in the world has been seeking the answer to this very question! So don't feel bad, you're not alone and you're in good company! In fact, there are very few people if any born to this world who never reach this point in their lives, no matter how well off they are financially and or relationally.
That is by design by the way!
I'm sure many of you have heard the notion that we are all born with an emptiness in our soul, a vacuum that can only be filled by a certain truth, or ideology, or a relationship with God. There is truth in that notion, however it goes much deeper than that and

the details will surprise you! So, let's get into those details.

Details

Some believe the meaning of life is to grow up, get married, have kids, and carry on your line. Others believe the meaning of life is to go full blast and have all the fun you can before you either get too old to do that anymore, or you die. Some believe that they are on a crusade of sorts to better humanity for their progeny in the next generation. Though these are all valid paths in life, they are not the meaning of life. The meaning of life is wrapped up in who we are and why we are here. I know, I have a knack for the obvious and you didn't need to buy this book to figure that out! Still, I urge you to bear with me because it does get much more interesting.

In order to fully understand the answer to the question that is the title of this book, I'm going to take you on a journey. One that is not only historical, but spiritual in nature as well. If you don't believe in things spiritual, I would encourage that you finish reading this book anyway. It may give you some insight that you might not have considered before. What the heck, if you're at this point in your life, it certainly can't hurt!

A Problem Arises

This journey I am referring to, starts before the world was created. It starts with a Father. This Father has one Son, but he wants more children. The capacity of this Father to love is so great, that he decides he is going to have more children. Many children mind you. As many as want to become his children. As many as the stars in the sky!
First things first though. This Father, whom I am referring to I'm sure you have guessed by now is God, and for reasons you will see, He has been described in most literature as the Heavenly Father. This very description speaks to his personality and desires, and helps us to personalize Him, and to identify more with Him. Now according to literature and scripture alike, God already had a host of angels who sang his praises and did his bidding with no questions asked and no rebellion whatsoever. However, this was not enough! For a being that goes by the description of Father, mere creations could

never be enough to satisfy the desire for offspring. So, a plan was made. A plan that would bring about the family this Father wanted and would at the same time be a family that was actually a part of Himself. I mean that is the distinction of real family is it not? To have children that are a part of yourself, of your own blood. Except in this case, Gods children would be of his own Spirit.
Now this plan had some very specific steps that had to take place for it to be successful, as well as morally just.
So, the first step of the plan was to create another angel, a special angel mind you, the most beautiful and powerful angel God had ever created and why God did this first, will soon become evident.
So, God creates this perfect angel. (By the way, this is all in scripture you just need to connect the dots.)
He names this perfect angel Lucifer and calls him the son of the morning. Lucifer was beautiful, he was powerful, but he lacked something that would prevent him from having a real relationship with God. That something was free will. If a person, or a

creation does not have free will, there can be no relationship. The basis of every proper relationship must always start with free will. Without it, all you have is one side exploiting the other side. All relationships must start with both sides choosing the other. Or not choosing!

So, God gave Lucifer free will. God new that without free will it would be impossible for Lucifer to have a reciprocal relationship with God like a family member would be able to do. Something more than just creator and creation.

I'm not sure if the creating of Lucifer was a test of sorts so that God could see what would happen if He put free will into a created being, or if God knew what would happen and was simply putting together pieces to a puzzle He had created in His mind. Given the fact that the Bible says that certain events took place before the foundation of the world, events that had not yet happened here on earth, I believe that God knew what would happen and He set the stage so to speak based on His foreknowledge. I also know that God didn't want another being that just did what they were created to do. Another being that just lived by instinct, or programming. He had that already in the many angels He had previously created. Oh, it was nice and all, these creatures singing and praising Him all of the time, but it did not fulfill the desire God had for a reciprocal love. The kind of love within families. That kind of love can only exist from a person or a being that has the free will to make the choice to do so.

Most people know parts of this story, some know all of it from either Sunday school or a family member. As the story goes, Lucifer exercised his free will by rebelling against God, instead of loving Him back as a son would. In fact, he actually tried to overthrow God and steal His kingdom! Did this reaction sound familiar to you? Many people today either try to create God in their own image, or they flat out deny His existence and set themselves up as their own God! There is a reason for this, and you will soon understand why this is with some people.

Now, God could have reacted by destroying Lucifer, however Instead of just destroying him, God made a plan to take a bad situation and use it for good. God was bound and determined to have many children, and He figured out a way to use Lucifer in this endeavor so that creating Lucifer was not a complete loss. In fact, Lucifer was a very large part in God's plan to birth children. So much so that the job probably couldn't get done without him!

One thing God learned through his experience with Lucifer was that giving a created being free will, without also giving that creation a part of himself, pretty much stacked the odds against the creation exercising their free will in a positive way because they didn't have Gods nature in them motivating them in that direction. So, God had to come up with another way to get a part of Himself into the creation, into mankind, in a way that it would happen by the choice, and not forced upon them by Himself.

The problem that God faced with placing a part of Himself in the mankind was the need for them to have the free will to begin with, in order for the gift, or the birthing if you will, to be legitimate. So how does God get His nature in us, so that our free will would lean toward choosing God? This was a problem!

Solving The Problem

One thing about God, is He is true to His nature, and His nature is one of pure love and trustworthiness as well as just. He is also a gentleman. You see God could not just place His seed in mankind and still be true to Himself. Why not you ask? He is God, He can do anything He wants! The answer is actually simple, that would be the same as rape and God is not a rapist. A rapist forces a person against their will into a most personal and intimate act where they place a part of themself in that person. Or they take something personal from that person without their consent. So, God had to figure out a way to give creation a choice to either decide they want to be a part of His family, or not.
In the Bible, it tells us that God chose us to be in Christ from before the foundation of the world.

Ephesians 1:3-5 KJV
[3] Blessed be the God and Father of our Lord Jesus Christ, who hath blessed us with all spiritual blessings in heavenly places in Christ:

[4] According as he hath chosen us in him before the foundation of the world, that we should be holy and without blame before him in love: [5] Having predestinated us unto the adoption of children by Jesus Christ to himself, according to the good pleasure of his will,

What does this mean?   By the way, in verse 5 where the writer speaks of predestination, it does not mean that God predestined some to be His children and others not to be. The predestination spoken of here is regards to the method by which He brings people into His family and that method is by His Son, and in His Son, Jesus Christ. There is no other way, God predestined the method to be in Christ. So, what does that mean? What does it mean to be in Christ, and to have Christ in us? In a nutshell it means to have the very life and nature of God in us. This is what the scriptures mean when they speak of being reborn by the incorruptible seed. This is what makes us acceptable to God as children, birthed by His nature, His life.
Religion on the other hand would have us believe that our acceptance by God is based on our actions, or our ability to be moral. You

see God knew we couldn't be moral in and of ourselves, based on the reaction of Lucifer after he received free will. What does Lucifers actions have to do with ours you ask? His actions have everything to do with ours for one specific reason, we are born with Lucifers nature! So, it makes perfect sense that we will tend to act out as he did. Not necessarily a guarantee, but a tendency. How do I know we are born with Lucifers nature? Well for one Jesus said so! Ever hear of when the group of religious pharisees we're trying set up Jesus so He would be killed? Jesus told them that they were acting like they were because their father the devil was a murderer from the beginning! I get deeper into this truth a little later so hang in there.

Religion vs The Birthing

There is a difference between Gods plan for mankind, and religion. Religion has always required the efforts of man to reach out to God in their own efforts and to be counted righteous and acceptable by those actions. It is that way in every religion that has ever existed with the exception of Christianity. Christianity teaches that God, after creating mankind, reached out to us and first, proved that we could not please Him with our actions and our offerings. It goes much deeper than that as you will soon read. God did this through the law. The law was not something to live by so much as it was something to prove to us that we were not righteous enough to live by it, and that we needed assistance. Not that the law was bad or anything like that, it's just that no one can obey the law fully for one, and the law cannot birth children. It can only expose sin. It cannot give life, and it was and is Gods ultimate goal to give us life. Not just life in the sense of living, but life in the sense of His life, everlasting life.

So, God figured out a way for mankind to become acceptable, not by anything man could do, but because of what God did. In other words, in Christianity, God provides the way, the truth and the life, with no effort from mankind, so that mankind can become one with God in Jesus Christ. That is why Jesus told his disciples,

"I am the way, the truth, and the life, no one comes to the Father, but by me."

The Father He was referring to is God the Father. Jesus himself is God the Son. He is the first-born Son of God the scriptures say and is one with God! I can't really explain that dynamic. The scriptures do not tell us how He became the first born but it does say He has always been with God and in God the Father. Other religions reject the ideology of Jesus being God in the flesh. Not only is He the Son of God, but He was God who became a man, and the reason He became a man in body, was to reconcile us to God.
It really is as simple as that! The problem with people who are steeped in religion, or secular humanism, is the belief that one can basically

be their own god! It is the simplicity of Gods way that becomes a stumbling block to them! We want to feel like we had something to do with our own redemption. Complete trust in another is difficult for us because of our nature, a nature that we received from someone other than God.

The Way

There is a way that we can become children of God. That way is by belief, and belief alone! No other religion can make that statement. Every other religion in the world, with the exception of atheism and secular humanism, require a person to adopt a belief in a system of physical acts such as performing rituals, and or praying a certain way or meditating or any outward act that claims to be a way to appease God. It's always about appeasing a righteous God in other religions. Worshiping Him in certain prescribed ways and has nothing to do with becoming an actual child of God.
Analogies break down but Christianity would be like a father watching his child work and work to achieve the completion of a project and fail time and again. So, this father steps in having the expertise to complete the project and he does just that. Even though the father completed the project, the entire benefit of that project belongs to the child,

with no help from the child. Yet the child gets to enjoy the benefits of the fathers work on that project!

Now let's get into explaining just how God set things up and accomplished this miracle of giving spiritual life to anyone who wants it, with no religious effort on their own. The Way!

Creation

The first thing God needed to do was create mankind. Remember, He already created Lucifer and we know how that turned out. One thing about Lucifer, is he was not created in the image and likeness of God. Lucifer was created an Angel. The first angel in fact to receive free will that we know of. He was, according to scripture, very beautiful and powerful.
So, God decided to create mankind differently. He created the first man in His own image and likeness according to the scriptures. I believe this to mean that since God is tripartite, meaning he is one God, but He manifests Himself in three persons. Those persons, or personalities are,

Father
Son
Holy Spirit

He created man with,

A Body
A soul
And Spiritual capacity

Each personality of the God head, Father, Son and Spirit, ministers to a different part of this new creation God called man. Sometimes the Godhead personalities will overlap for example it is written that God the Son is co-creator of the universe with God the Father as God the Father is creator of all. So, they share that task and ability.
God the Son is the sacrifice for the sins of the world, and He is the life of the believer. He by the way, agreed to do this before the world was even created, according to scripture. Now He shares being the life of the believer with God the Father but being the sacrifice for the sins of the world is solely the responsibility of God the Son. He bears that responsibility himself 100%.
God the Holy Spirit is the teacher, or revealer of these truths.
Many people struggle with the concept of God manifesting himself in three personalities. I have debated with Muslims especially who consider this concept ungodly,

even blasphemous! I have attempted to explain this doctrine to them by reminding them that they operate similarly! For example, a man is a son to his father, and if he has children he is also a father. If he is married, he is also a husband. 3 personalities in one person. So far, I have yet to be successful in getting a Muslim to accept that logic! They believe that God can be understood through science and logic. This is untrue as I hope to reveal, so please continue with me.

So, God the Father created man from dirt the scriptures tell us. Basically, He took some clay and made a figurine to the shape and size that He wanted. He then breathed the breath of life into that figurine turning it into flesh and giving it the ability to function, to breathe, and to think.

Now let me explain that the breath of life spoken of here, is not spiritual life. It is the ability of the creation to function, to breath and to think. Spiritual life is something completely different and in fact existed long before physical life ever came to be.

God then created in man a capacity for a spirit. This is where we are different from animals and other creatures here on earth that

God created. Animals do not have spiritual capacity. They have only body and soul. They are not body, soul and spirit like mankind is because God did not create animals and other creatures in His image. There is a scripture that says, "God is all and is in all." However, that just means that all life comes from and is supported by God, and what is in all, is the breath of life, not necessarily spiritual life. God then decided that this man He created in His image needed a companion. A companion that differed from man a bit. So, the scriptures say that God put this man whom He named Adam into a deep sleep and performed surgery in him. He removed one rib from Adam, and He then created for Adam another being that in some ways was opposite of Adam, and God called that being female, and named her Eve. God then gave them both free will, just like He did with Lucifer. Eve, like Adam had a body and a soul, but was still void in spirit just like Adam. So now here they were, both with a body, and a soul, and spiritual capacity, and they had free will. The spirit part of Adam and Eve was the part that would hopefully house Gods Spirit one day. This part of man, along with the soul, are the two most important parts of us. By the way, the soul, is our mind, will and emotions. It is the part of us that is our personality and intellect. It contains our memories and thought processes and what makes us different from other people. It is easy to mistake the soul for the spirit, but they are two different parts of our creation. Like I said before, mankind is the only physical creation with spiritual capacity along with their body and soul. Therefore, I believe that this is what it means to be created in Gods image and likeness. The animals and all other forms of creation with the exception of angelic spiritual beings, have only a body and a soul, and their soul motivates them by instinct, rather than by a spirit and free will like ours does. The angelic spiritual beings have a spirit and a soul rather than a body and a soul. They are all two-part creations instead of three like mankind. This is important to understand as you will see.

The problem for God was getting His Spirit into mankind's spirit part without forcing it upon them. Based on our society and morals, which originated with God, for God to just place His spirit in man without consent, would be considered rape. This most intimate act that God could ever do, to place His seed, His spirit into mankind but that act had to be consensual, and as of yet, Adam and Eve had no idea of the magnitude or understanding of any of this.

The Stage

So, God is finished with creation, but now He must figure a way to get His Spirit into the part of man that is made to contain it.
Let me back up for just a minute though and explain why God is doing all of this!
The Bible says,
For God so loved the world... let me stop right there. I want to remind you that God is inherently a lover. As well, the scriptures often use the term Father, when referring to Him. When using the term Father, the scriptures are giving us a glimpse into His character. What makes a father a father? Children of course! This is what God is after. This is His end game. To have many children. Children are His motivation. One could even guess that even the God of the universe wants companionship and desires that intimacy that only family can provide. The very concept of family originated with God. God has had angels and other beings like the angels for eons singing His praises

and doing His bidding. It's not the same as having His own children, however. I know that may sound simplistic, God being the creator of the universe and all, but that is His motivation. There are other parts to this whole system, for example believers in Christ are referred to as the bride of Christ. More family connotations! Are you starting to see the connection? God is family oriented. The concept of family is ingrained in mankind from creation because of this attribute.

Now let's get back to the stage. Remember, Gods dilemma is getting His spiritual seed into mankind without going against the free will He put in man. This was a risky endeavor to say the least! I remember one day my wife's son complaining to her about his chores and responsibilities. He made the comment that he didn't ask to be born, so why does he have to have all these responsibilities?
You see if God would have just placed His seed in man, these type complaints could have been serious issues. Not only that, but God has certain attributes that cannot be infringed even by Himself! He will not go against who He is and His nature just to

obtain what He wants. There are certain rules, rules of morality, of justice and propriety that must be strictly adhered to because He is God! This is the reason for His elaborate plan on how to get a part of Himself into man without using force or perversion to do it. He knew it would be possible that many would become so ingrained into their first nature, that they may not accept Him. However, to stay true to Himself, this was the only way. So, He created a garden. In this garden everything was perfect, and beautiful and not subjected to corruption or decay, thorns or weeds or anything like that. He placed Adam and Even in this garden to live. He even made himself available to them on a daily basis and walked with them in the cool of the mornings. Wow! Think about it! God and man during this time walked together and talked together and visited with each other in this perfect garden that God created. You would think that this is it! How could it get any better? The problem is, things were not as God wanted them yet, and they were not in the best interests of mankind either believe it or not!

Adam and Eve were there because God placed them there. Not because they chose to be there. They had free will, but they had not yet used it. You will understand why in a bit. So, every day God showed up and walked with His creation, when what He really wanted was to walk with His birthed children who loved Him as much as He loved them. Adam and Eve at this point did not love God. They didn't even understand the concept of love, and though everything in the garden was perfect, it wasn't family yet.

The Fall

Now everything in the garden was at the disposal of Adam and Eve, with one exception. In that garden God placed a tree. There were actually many trees in the garden, but this particular tree God said was special, and they were not to eat of it. He then warned them that if they did eat of that tree, they would die that very day. This tree was called 'The Tree of the Knowledge of Good and Evil'. In all reality it was just a fruit tree! There wasn't anything special to this tree in the physical sense, like it had magical properties or anything like that. God could have used avocados, or bananas or anything really! It was what this tree represented to Adam and Eve in their own minds that made it significant. This is history's first recorded law, or thou shalt not!
The warning came with it a substantial consequence as you will see. The consequence was death! As we press on you

will see exactly what kind of death God meant.

The significance wasn't so much in the tree as it was in the minds of Adam and Eve. You can take any object, tell people it's forbidden, and something happens in our minds! We are drawn to the very thing that is forbidden. Now there is no indication that this psychological phenomenon was happening in Adam and Eve, yet. It couldn't yet because remember, a part of their creation was not complete yet. Something had to take place for that psychological phenomenon to become an issue, or a weakness in mankind and it was about to happen! Evil was the missing ingredient needed for their free will to be of any use. Free will is a moot point without the existence of both good and evil! Give someone free will, yet only give them good stimulus, then a true choice can never be made. Evil must accompany good for free will to operate.

So, God created evil!

Isaiah 45:7 KJV

[7] I form the light, and create darkness: I make peace, and create evil: I the Lord do all these things.

We must understand that God is not evil, even though He created it. Remember, He created Lucifer, and by Lucifer's own choice he became evil. This is why God did not destroy Lucifer right away. He used him for this purpose, to bring evil to the world so that there would be the contrast to good so that mankind could exercise free will.
Adam and Eve exercised free will for the first time in the history of the world the day Lucifer showed up and deceived them.

The Awakening!

So here we are in the garden of Eden. The stage is set for what is about to happen next. Adam and Eve have been wandering the garden for who knows how long, the scriptures aren't clear about that. Many scholars believe it was but a mere couple of hours they spent in the garden before the fall. We do not know exactly, but they are meeting with God and enjoying all that there is in this garden. They had no clue they were naked, there were no inhibitions or evil thoughts, no lying no stealing or anything of that nature going on in Eden, yet! One might even say, well why didn't God leave it like that? It was perfect! The problem is, according to God and unbeknownst to man, it was not perfect. Adam and Eve didn't love God. They didn't even know what love was. Up until then there had never been any contrast to all the good that was in the garden. So even though they had free will, the occasion to exercise that free will in a way contrary to Gods wishes had not yet happened, and until it did, love could not exist.

You see, loving someone is based not only on feelings for someone, but also on being committed to them even in the face of temptations and distractions. Nothing had happened in the garden to create those scenarios, yet!

The Deceiver

This is where Lucifer comes in! Remember him? The fallen Angel with free will who tried to usurp Gods throne and kingdom? One day, we don't know how long after God set up the garden, Satan showed up. He was disguised as the most beautiful creature in the garden, a serpent. At that time serpents had legs and feet. I believe they looked more like a beautiful dragon than today's serpent.
I would like to point out here that Lucifer showed up at a time when both Adam and God were not present, and he showed up when Eve was near the tree of the knowledge of good and evil. Eve was by herself doing whatever she was doing when she saw him, and when Lucifer saw that she noticed his beauty and looked, he struck up a conversation with her.
Eventually the conversation led him to ask her about the tree with the beautiful fruit nearby. Eve explained to the serpent, that particular tree was off limits and that God said

it would kill them if they ate from it. Whatever kill meant I'm sure she didn't understand, she had never seen or experienced death before, so she had nothing to compare it to. For all she knew it could just mean a stopped-up nose or something else as minor! I don't believe that she even understood that it was something bad! How could she? Death, sickness, or any other kind of ailment had never before come upon them. Given that truth, I can see how easily it must have been for Lucifer to deceive her.

Lucifer smiled and almost laughed, he kind of chuckled to himself, telling her that surely God was either mistaken or He had lied to them! He got her to look at how beautiful the fruit looked and assured her it was even better to eat. Not only that, but he also convinced her that God was most likely holding out on them, knowing that if they ate the fruit, they would be like God and would know everything! They would be as smart as God and God didn't want that.

So, Eve, not having any experience with deception or any kind of wrongdoing, didn't know to be wary and listened to Lucifers speech. She wound up believing his lies and at his invitation, she ate some of the fruit. Eve then went to Adam and fed him some of the same fruit.

I would like to talk about the dynamics of this encounter for a minute and point out some observations of mine regarding how Lucifer operates, and how men and women often interact. I would like to point out some of the tactics Lucifer used when he deceived Eve. First, he disguised himself. We often think of Satan as looking like an evil long horned animal snarling with blood and spittle coming from his mouth, or something of that nature. That's actually not the case! Lucifer wants to attract people, not repel them. The Bible says that he disguises himself as an angel of light, and his ministers disguise themselves as ministers of light! It's important to understand that Satan will make himself appealing. He wants to attract, not scare away.

Next, he waited until both God and Adam were not around before he approached Eve in the garden. Satan is not stupid. He knew somehow that the woman most likely had more influence over the man than he would have. Eve was probably beautiful, and Adam was most likely enamored by her! Lucifer used Eve to get to both of them because of the differences between men and women. Women tend to be more emotional, and they are usually captivated by beautiful things. Men are captivated by women! It doesn't take a genius to see why Lucifer went about his deception the way he did.

Third, Lucifer went after all of Eve's senses when he began his deception. The lust of the flesh, that fruit tastes good, the lust of the eyes, it is beautiful to behold, the pride of life, you can be your own god! This is Lucifers MO. He is very good at what he does, and for this reason, God did not destroy him! Instead, God kept him to be a tool in Gods toolbox. God used Satan as a way for evil to come to the world so that the free will He gave mankind would be legitimately operated.

A Tool in The Shed

Remember when I wrote that God figured out a purpose for Lucifer rather than destroy him?
There had to be a contrast to good, so that Adam and Eve would have something opposite to compare it to to make an informed decision. All that they had to choose from in the garden was good! Because of that, free will was useless. Evil had to come into the world! Free will must have both good and evil present for it to be a valid trait. If there were only good, or only evil, there would be no need for free will. Without both, there are no choices to be made.
The old Yin and Yang theory from eastern philosophy is a true philosophy. The working together of good and evil is necessary for us to exercise free will. Without both, free will is useless.
Most religions have aspects of truth to them. In fact, the closer a doctrine is to the

truth, without being fully true, the more dangerous a philosophy or a religion it is! I am of course talking about religions that deny Jesus Christ.

God had a pretty good idea that Adam and Eve would go the same way that Lucifer did, so in His wisdom, He came up with a plan that though in the beginning it would cause the fall of man, in the end, it would bring about mankind's reconciliation to God, and with it, mankind's salvation.

This plan included using Lucifer to fill the need for good to have its opposite, which is evil. Like I said earlier, Lucifer is nothing more than a tool in Gods shed so to speak. He is also the current spiritual ruler of this world! It is Lucifers job to deceive and to wreak havoc on society. To be the black, in the Yin and Yang.

I know this must sound very fairy tale-ish! However, I assure you, this is all real. These are historical facts, put together by connecting the dots in scripture, along with the Spirit of God providing revelation. If you're a believer in Jesus Christ, you will begin to understand what I am writing. If you're not, you may think this is way out there. The thing you must think of is, why do you have that eternal perspective, and why are you seeking the meaning to life? I encourage you to read on, give this some time to soak in. If you are sincere about wanting to know the meaning of life, I believe things will begin to make sense. Now back to the subject.

The Result of Evil

The result of Adam and Eve believing Lucifer in the garden is that they received his spirit into the part of them that God had created for spiritual capacity. That part of us that makes us spiritual beings, and not just flesh and thought.
Sounds crazy, doesn't it? How do I know that this is what happened? What makes me so sure about this truth that I am willing to bet my life on it? Remember when I said understanding scripture is about connecting the dots in many cases? It's true, sometimes you must bounce back and forth in the scriptures to put together a truth. One of those dots is in the New Testament, in the book of John. Jesus was talking to a group of Pharisees. One of the topics they were discussing was where Jesus came from, and who His father was, as well as who the historical father of these Jewish leaders was. When Jesus made it clear that He was the one sent from God the Father and was in

fact Gods Son, many Jews believed, but some did not and sought to kill Him for His words. They claimed that their historical father was Abraham, and because of that, they felt that their father was ultimately God! Jesus told them that if their father was God, that they wouldn't be seeking to kill Him. Then He told them that their true father, the devil, was the murderer from the beginning and that they were his offspring because they sought to kill him!
According to these Pharisees, these Jewish religious leaders, Jesus was committing blasphemy! Which based on the law, could be punishable by death! Here is that account as recorded in the book of John.

John 8:37-44 KJV
[37] I know that ye are Abraham's seed; but ye seek to kill me, because my word hath no place in you. [38] I speak that which I have seen with my Father: and ye do that which ye have seen with your father. [39] They answered and said unto him, Abraham is our father. Jesus saith unto them, If ye were Abraham's children, ye would do the works of Abraham. [40] But now ye seek to kill me, a man that hath told you the

truth, which I have heard of God: this did not Abraham. [41] Ye do the deeds of your father. Then said they to him, We be not born of fornication; we have one Father, even God. [42] Jesus said unto them, If God were your Father, ye would love me: for I proceeded forth and came from God; neither came I of myself, but he sent me. [43] Why do ye not understand my speech? even because ye cannot hear my word. [44] Ye are of your father the devil, and the lusts of your father ye will do. He was a murderer from the beginning, and abode not in the truth, because there is no truth in him. When he speaketh a lie, he speaketh of his own: for he is a liar, and the father of it.

John also recorded that Jesus, though He loved mankind, He did not trust mankind because He knew what was in them.

John 2:24-25 KJV
[24] But Jesus did not commit himself unto them, because he knew all men, [25] And needed not that any should testify of man: for he knew what was in man.

This is how I can be so confident in what I am writing regarding mankind's spiritual state before belief in Christ. These words of Jesus were recorded by the apostle John. Every single human being ever born since Adam, has Lucifers spirit of sin and death indwelling them in their spirit part.

Jesus, being the Son of God, and co-creator of the universe and all that is in it, knew better than anyone what was in mankind. If we never know anything else, this truth alone answers so many questions regarding the state of this world. It explains why people are by nature evil. It explains why young babies do not have to be taught how to lie, steal, or harm others. They in fact must be taught NOT to do those things! It explains why there is always conflict in this world and it is the reason why that will never change. We will never take this world for Christ because right now it belongs to the devil! He is the father of every person except those who have believed in Jesus.

We struggle as a society to build a world that is safe and free from corruption and violence. Never understanding that the deck is stacked against us because a large part of the world population is motivated by a nature that is corrupt and evil in nature. Christianity is the only religion that offers its followers new life, a new nature, right now! Not in some pie in the sky future tense. Every other religion in the entire world, can only offer rules, laws, ceremonies, and other carnal physical ways to appease a god that cannot do anything for anyone about their evil nature. No other religion can fix mankind's nature. Some of these other religions only offer an ideology that says you can be your own god, or there is no god, and after you die all is for nothing! Some religions teach reincarnation as a truth, and if you don't get it right this time, you will come back as some other creature and can work your way back to being a human after having been various other creatures!

The very worst of these other religions, attempt to get people to believe that Satan, is the god they should be worshiping, instead of the God who created Satan! They do not understand that Satan is nothing more than a tool in Gods toolbox, and that he is here temporarily bringing evil to the world, so that free will can exist. That is his job, to deceive, and bring evil and chaos to the world.

New Life and Understanding

In contrast, Jesus promises new life. This new life is the spiritual birthing of the life and nature of God and is available to anyone who believes in Jesus Christ and places their trust in Him. He is the only one who can make new, the spirit within us.

We cannot understand all of this until we believe in Christ. All that we have the ability to know and understand, is the basic premise that we are by nature sinners, no matter how good we act. That is our conscience. It is in mankind's nature to be evil, and we can feel bad about it! Problem is, on our own we can do nothing about it! Sure, we can exercise self-control and willpower to a certain degree, some can completely! But we cannot fix the problem. The evil nature is still within us. The only way our inner evil can be shed, is through Christ Jesus. I know I mentioned this already, but I'm going to bring it up again. It is sometimes difficult for people who are generally good people, you know, people who do not express their evil nature like others might, to come to the realization that they need a savior. Evil does not always manifest itself in bad behavior! When we think of evil most of us tend to visualize murder, theft, adultery, and rape and the like. Evil can also disguise itself as good believe it or not! That is exactly what Lucifer did in the garden to Eve.

The good news is, that once we take the step and believe, and trust in Christ to eradicate the old sin nature, He rebirths us into Gods family by replacing that evil nature with His own nature! One of the byproducts of that miracle, is that we can now understand Gods mysteries!

You see the only truth a person can understand prior to the rebirth, is the truth that they are a sinner and that they need a savior. That is all that God will allow anyone to understand until they take that step of faith and believe. That is why we see so many debates between Christian's and non-Christians that do not get anywhere. The way God has designed the revealing of truth, is

that the unbeliever can only come to the knowledge of their sin and recognize the need for a savior before they become a believer. They cannot understand the deep mysteries of God and how and why He chose to do things the way He does them.
Why does God do that? Wouldn't it be easier if He gave us understanding first so that we could decide based on knowledge rather than faith? In a sense It would be easier, however the problem remains that only life can understand life, just as death understands death. In order for us to even be able to understand the mysteries of God, we must have God in us, and He cannot put a part of Himself in us without our permission. That is why Gods whole system is set up the way that it is. It really couldn't be any other way. I have searched for truth most of my adult life. I have considered other possible ways God could have done things differently. This way, Gods way in Christ is the only way God could get what He is looking for at the level His nature requires. Yes, it's true! God must be true to His nature! He cannot do anything that would go against who He is. This is one of the big differences between God and

Lucifer. God would not place His seed in mankind without their permission. He is a gentleman, He is righteous, and He is true to himself. Lucifer on the other hand, is no better than a common thief or murderer or rapist! He is the father of such attributes and used deception to get his seed into mankind. Who do you want to trust your eternal life and soul to?

Recap

Now let's recap what we have so far. God created man and gave him free will. However, because evil had not yet entered the garden, which was the place that God set up for Adam and Eve to live in after their creation. Though they had free will, it was never used in the garden until Lucifer showed up because everything was good there. Evil did not introduce itself until then. No one really knows how long Adam and Eve lived in Eden until Lucifer arrived. It could have been an hour, it could have been one day, it could have been thousands of years. No one knows for sure. I don't believe time as we know it started until after Adam and Eve were expelled from the garden anyway.

Once evil was introduced to their lives through Lucifers deception, not only was free will now able to be exercised, because both good and evil were available to choose from, Adam and Eve now began to experience a knowledge that they did not possess before! They now knew they were naked, and they experienced shame as they hid from God as a result of that shame.

When God later showed up for their regular walk in the garden, He questioned them about it, and for the first time ever, blame and lies began to flow from the mouths of Adam and Eve! This was the result of the evil nature that had entered their spirit after believing Lucifer. It was automatic! They couldn't help it. How many times have we heard from some criminal the words, "I couldn't seem to help myself!" Serial killers all spoke of a compulsion that they could not seem to control. That compulsion stems from the sin nature they received from Lucifer. For many years I understood that we had a sin nature before we believed in Jesus Christ. However, it never dawned on me until just the last couple of years who that nature came from and how we got it. Most believe that it just entered man when Adam and Eve disobeyed God, which it did, however understanding that it came directly from Lucifer, is not something that is mainstream evangelical teaching.

It makes sense to me that we can conclude from this experience, along with other information in the scriptures, such as Jesus saying that a person cannot enter the kingdom of heaven unless they are born again, born of the incorruptible seed, that spiritual birthing's come about as a result of believing a spiritual entity! Connecting the dots in scripture to me, solidifies this theory. This is exactly what happened to Adam and Eve in the garden when they believed Lucifer and did not believe God. I can think of no other plausible explanation as to how they got Satan's spirit in them as Jesus made inference to in the book of John.

This theory ties in perfectly with all the scriptures in the Bible that point to how mankind managed to wind up with the spirit of sin and death in them, and Jesus telling the Pharisees that they were of their father the devil, drives that point home!

So, at this point in history, we have a fallen mankind, with a nature that is evil, and in need of salvation from that nature.

The Plan

Now that we understand how mankind received in them a sin nature, or rather, a Satan nature, because it was in fact Satan's nature they received, how does mankind get himself out of this terrible situation that they are in?
Sadly, we cannot get ourselves out this situation. We need help. We cannot on our own crawl out of the pit we wound up in when our ancestor's believed an evil and corrupt spiritual being, whose sole purpose was and is to deceive and destroy Gods special creation. How do we reverse this spiritual birthing that took place in our progenitors when they believed the serpent instead of God? What a dilemma! However, it was a dilemma that God had already thought through and provided an answer to before He even created the world!

I wish to interject here that what I am writing in this book is not fantasy! These are historical events as recorded in the bestselling book that has ever been written and sold, the

Bible. Some of you by now are scoffing and thinking how ridiculous I sound by writing this book and espousing in it what I have come to believe as absolute fact. Some of you believe what I am saying because you have already wrestled with notion of the Bible and its validity and have come away from that wrestling match with a solid belief in its validity.

Whether you believe the Bible to be factual or not, one thing still remains, no one in the history of the world has come up with a better answer to the questions we all have in our minds regarding who we are, why we are here, and what is the meaning to life! No other writer or philosopher has even come close to creating a work such as the Bible.

I know the argument!

"Man wrote the Bible, so it is filled with errors."

Yes, men wrote all the books and letters that make up what we call the Bible today. The difference between these works and most other books on the shelf, is that the books of the Bible are inspired by God Himself. He inspired and motivated each writer whose book or epistle made it into the cannon of scripture. The Bible itself makes this claim!

2 Timothy 3:16 KJV
[16] All scripture is given by inspiration of God, and is profitable for doctrine, for reproof, for correction, for instruction in righteousness:

Now, I don't expect anyone to just up and believe what I say about the scriptures to be true. However, there is one bit of information that in my opinion gives the Bible the credibility that so many say it has. The resurrection. The whole history of Jesus that is written in the Bible is backed up by that one event, and I mean to tell you, that's one heck of an event! The fact that Jesus rose from the dead and was seen by over 500 people begs attention! Were it not for the resurrection, the whole historical documentation that is in the Bible would definitely be up for scrutiny. Nevertheless, Jesus did raise from the dead. So, there is that!
Now, back to what I was writing about.
I think Satan at this point probably thought to himself that he had done something irreversible to Gods special creation! He

didn't know that God had planned this out and executed it in His mind before the foundation of the world was ever laid!
Satan's whole purpose since his own fall has been to drag others down with him and to destroy anything relating to God. This is his nature, this is how he operates, and we can substantiate this theory further by noting that this is also the nature of human
beings. Misery loves company they say! How many times in your own life have you had someone you know, or love try to drag you into their problems, their sin, or their addiction? Or how many times have we ourselves, done that to others?
The mind and nature of an evil person will try to drag others down with them because sin and death is a lonely state!
Now you need to understand that I am speaking of human beings in general. Some are born into this world with a stronger will power or ability to curb the sin nature in them better than others. It is these people who often have the harder time realizing that they are inherently evil! It is even more difficult for them to realize that they are no better than

anyone else because of the sin nature that is in them.

Not always, but often a sense of self-righteousness prevents some people from understanding truths such as this. They think, I'm a good person! I've never hurt anyone; I don't lie or steal or do anything bad to anyone. Why do I need a savior? Surely God will not reject me I've been a good person! They do not understand that the issue has to do with the nature that is in us, and not our actions.

I get it, when you have lived your life, not giving in outwardly to evil thoughts, and to desires of the flesh, sometimes not even having thoughts like that at all, it can be frustrating to watch others seemingly not care and give in to those thoughts and temptations. There is even a parable in the Bible depicting this behavior. It is the parable of the prodigal son. A story of a father with two sons. One son is a good son, he works hard and does as his father asks, never giving his father grief. The other son is restless and wild. He goes to his father demanding his inheritance so he can go out into the world. His father sadly gives it to him because he knows this sons attitude and behavior will not change and hopes the world will be a lesson that will change his youngest sons attitude and wildness. So, the wild son takes off into the world and moves away from his father and everything he knows. He winds up spending all his inheritance on wild parties, drinking and gambling and just having fun. One day he wakes up with bad hangover and realizes he has partied his whole inheritance away! After a couple days without eating and living on the streets he becomes desperate and begins looking for a job. All he could find was a job feeding and caring for a pig farmer's pigs. He reasons in his mind that at least he will be able to share the scraps of food the pigs eat while he cares for them. Basically, he has hit rock bottom. One day he realizes that his life has gotten pretty bad, so he decides to humble himself and go home and see if his father will take him back in and at least allow him to work for his keep. Even if it meant sleeping in the barn, anything would be better than where he was now.

After traveling for a few days, he arrived at his father's property and his father saw him walking down the path toward him and jumped up and ran to greet his son! He embraced his son and took him back in. He called to his servants to put together a great feast so they could celebrate the return of his beloved son. There was no judgmental I told you so or anything like that. The Father was truly happy that his son had come back home and was alive!

The older son, after watching his father's reaction went to his father and was upset! He asked his father why he was treating his brother so well after how he had left them and blown his inheritance! His father replied, my son was lost, and now he is found, praise God for this miracle! Yet the good son was still upset about his father's treatment of the prodigal son and felt cheated himself because he had never done anything like his brother had done.

There are several lessons in this parable, but the one that I want to point out here is the prodigal son's older brothers' anger at his father's reaction of love toward his younger brother. The older brother was angry because he had been good all his life and he had never had his father do this for him. He didn't realize that all that his father had was his! His

younger brothers' failures and his father's forgiveness of them, created in the older brother an angry, self-righteous attitude. His father replied to the older son, "you have always been with me, and all that I have is yours. It is proper that we rejoice for your brother, for your brother was lost, and now he is found, he was dead, and now is alive!"
The main point I want to make from this parable is the fact that whether we are good or bad, has no bearing on Gods decision to give us eternal life. Gods' acceptance of us has nothing to do with how we have lived our lives. Every human being is born with an evil sin nature in them. So, every human being, whether they have lived their life morally, or whether they have squandered everything and have committed sin after sin, has no bearing on whether they will be able to enter heaven because the problem is in mankind's nature, not in their actions. Sin is in everyone's nature, whether our actions reflect it. It is simply a byproduct of a much deeper spiritual problem.
So here we are, a fallen creation, and a loving God. Yet the two cannot come together

unless something bridges the spiritual gap between them.

Bridging The Gap

So, what's a loving God to do? He already knows that starting over would be fruitless. Odds are it would just happen again! He has tried twice now to impart free will to two different creations and they have both failed, and they wound up His adversaries.
So, God decided that since starting over would only bring more of the same, He would figure out a way to give His special creation, the one He created in His own image and likeness, a way back to Himself, right from the get-go! A way to bridge the spiritual gap that exists between Himself, and mankind.
One of the things God did when He created mankind, was to put in us a small measure of faith. The scriptures tell us this. This small measure of faith is unique to mankind and gives us the ability to override the sin nature, by our free will, just enough to be able to hear the message of God's grace and be able to exercise that faith and believe. We know this is the case because Jesus one day was in a crowd of people like He usually was, and a

woman was there who had what the scriptures call an issue of blood. It was a medical problem unique to women where she wouldn't stop bleeding, like a period that would never end. The passage goes that she reasoned in her mind that if she could just touch the hem of Jesus garment, then she would be healed. She had heard of him doing many miracles and believed that He was indeed the Messiah. So, she got close enough to do just that and behold, she was immediately healed! Jesus sensed power going from Him and asked who had touched Him. This woman did not deny that it was her and she knelt before Jesus and confessed. Jesus then said to her that her faith had made her whole and told her to go in peace.

Some interesting facts regarding that experience are one, many other people were there and were touching Jesus inadvertently just because they were all crowded together, yet none of them were healed as the woman was. Also, Jesus told her that her faith, had made her whole! This is significant because it denotes a dispensational period. I'll explain in a second what that means. He said it was HER faith, that made her whole!

The reason I point this out is because it contrasts with what the apostle Paul wrote regarding our faith after we believe. Paul said, (and I am Paraphrasing here), that when we believe in Jesus, our sin nature dies, and our new life that we live is Christ in us. Then he goes on to say that not only is our new life Christ in us, but our faith is no longer our old faith either, it is the faith of Christ in us!

What point am I trying to make here? I'm trying to help believers see that if they only understood the birthing of Christ in them, then they would also understand that they now operate by the faith of Christ as well, and if that woman's faith was strong enough to heal her by touching Jesus' robe, how much stronger is the faith of Christ that now dwells in all believers?

Also, why was it her faith at that time, that healed her, but now in this time period, it is the faith of Christ that now heals and sustains us?

Dispensations

Dispensations are periods of time that have a beginning and an end. With the exception of the final dispensation which will have no end. When it comes to God, there are several dispensational time periods where His dealings with mankind are different in one, than they are in another.
It's kind of like having children. When a child is born, as a parent you deal with that child a certain way. They are helpless so you must do everything for that child. Then they begin to grow and gradually as they get older there are several periods in their life in which you deal with them differently because of their age and level of maturity.
With God, there were several different dispensations where He dealt with and interacted with mankind differently. The following are the different dispensations throughout the history of the world, and how God dealt with mankind through them.

Innocence:

This dispensation covered the period of Adam and Eve in the Garden of Eden. In this dispensation God's commands were to (1) replenish the earth with children, (2) subdue the earth, (3) have dominion over the animals, (4) care for the garden, and (5) abstain from eating the fruit from the tree of knowledge of good and evil. God warned of the punishment of physical and spiritual death for disobedience. It is not clear scripturally whether Adam and Eve had children in the garden. The first recorded child was Cain, and he wasn't born until the second dispensation. Scripture seems to overlap between the first and second dispensations, meaning the story told is not necessarily in chronological order. It looks like Adam was given the go ahead to be fruitful and multiply and have dominion over all the animals in this the first dispensation, if that were the case, then any children they had during this time of innocence, must have eaten the fruit from the tree of the knowledge of good and evil as well, otherwise, Lucifers nature could not have entered them. I lean more toward the belief that they did not have children until the second dispensation, after they were cast out of the garden. Either way, the sin nature of Lucifer was birthed into mankind's spirit part during this dispensation. Most likely this dispensation did not last very long. In fact, it is possible it only lasted an hour or two!

Conscience:

This dispensation lasted from the time of Adam and Eve's eviction from the garden until the flood. This dispensation demonstrates what mankind will do if left to his own will and conscience, which have been tainted by the inherited sin nature. The five major aspects of this dispensation are 1) a curse on the serpent, 2) a change in womanhood and childbearing, 3) a curse on nature, 4) the imposing of difficult work on mankind to produce food, and 5) the promise of Christ as the seed who will bruise the serpent's head (Satan).
Let's talk about this for a minute. This is the first recorded hint if you will, of the seed of woman, and the serpent, Lucifer, and there being enmity between the two at some future date. Interesting note, the scriptures say that

it is the woman's seed, that will bring enmity to the serpent. This wording is a foreshadow of Gods Son becoming man! Otherwise, God would have said His own seed and not the woman's seed! "The woman's seed", was speaking of Jesus.

Human Government:

God had destroyed life on earth with a flood because of how evil it had become, saving just one family to restart humanity. God made the following promises and commands to Noah and his family:
1. God will not curse the earth again.
2. Noah and family are to replenish the earth with people.
3. They shall have dominion over the animal creation.
4. They are allowed to eat meat.
5. The law of capital punishment is established.
6. There never will be another worldwide flood.
7. The sign of God's promise will be the rainbow.

Noah's descendants did not scatter and fill the earth as God had commanded, thus failing in their responsibility in this dispensation. About 325 years after the flood, the earth's inhabitants began building a tower, a great monument to their solidarity and pride (Genesis 11:7-9). God brought the construction to a halt, creating different languages and enforcing His command to fill the earth. The result was the rise of different nations and cultures. From that point on, human governments have been a reality.

Promise:

This dispensation started with the call of Abraham, continued through the lives of the patriarchs, and ended with the Exodus of the Jewish people from Egypt. During this dispensation God developed a great nation that He had chosen as His people, the nation is Israel.

The basic promise during the Dispensation of Promise was the Abrahamic Covenant. Here are some of the key points of that unconditional covenant:

1. From Abraham would come a great nation that God would bless with natural and spiritual prosperity.
2. God would make Abraham's name great.
3. God would bless those that blessed Abraham's descendants and curse those that cursed them.
4. In Abraham all the families of the earth will be blessed. This is fulfilled in Jesus Christ and His work of salvation.
5. The sign of the covenant is circumcision.
6. This covenant, which was repeated to Isaac and Jacob, is confined to the Hebrew people and the 12 tribes of Israel.

Law:

It lasted almost 1,500 years, from the Exodus from Egypt, until it was suspended after Jesus Christ's death. This dispensation will start back up during the Millennium, with some modifications. During the Dispensation of Law, God dealt specifically with the Jewish nation through the Mosaic Covenant, or the Law, found in Exodus 19–23. The dispensation involved temple worship directed by priests, with further direction spoken through God's mouthpieces, the prophets. Eventually, due to the people's disobedience to the covenant, the tribes of Israel lost the Promised Land and were subjected to bondage.

Grace:

It began with the New Covenant in Christ's blood and continues today. Man's responsibility during the Dispensation of Grace is to believe in Jesus, the Son of God (John 3:18). In this dispensation the Holy Spirit indwells believers as the Comforter (John 14:16-26). This dispensation has lasted for almost 2,000 years, and no one knows when it will end. We do know that it will end with the Rapture of all born-again believers from the earth to go to heaven with Christ. Following the Rapture will be the judgments of God lasting for seven years.

Millennial Kingdom:

The seventh dispensation is called the Millennial Kingdom of Christ and will last for 1,000 years as Christ Himself rules on earth. This Kingdom will fulfill the prophecy to the Jewish nation that Christ will return and be their King. The only people allowed to enter the kingdom are the born-again believers from the Age of Grace, righteous survivors of the seven years of tribulation, and the resurrected Old Testament saints. No unsaved person is allowed access into this kingdom. Satan is bound during the 1,000 years. This period ends with the final judgment (Revelation 20:11-14). The old world is destroyed by fire, and the New Heaven and New Earth of Revelation 21 and 22 will begin.

The scriptures speak of one more dispensation. It is called,
The Dispensation of The Fullness of Times.

This is what the scriptures say about this dispensation.
Ephesians 1:10 KJV
[10] That in the dispensation of the fulness of times he might gather together in one all things in Christ, both which are in heaven, and which are on earth; even in him:

Now this may be the tail end of the seventh dispensation, or it may stand alone as the final one as we enter eternity. We do know that by the very name of it, it is the last one.

Conclusion

The reason I decided to bore you with that last chapter on dispensations, is because I believe it is crucial in understanding the mind of God. How can one know the meaning of life without knowing His mind? It can't be done. If there is no God, what would be the point in even seeking the meaning of life? When you die your gone! Hopefully this book has opened your eyes to the possibility that God exists, if you happen to be one who doesn't believe in God.
I know many of you may not have been looking for a book with this much scriptural reference, and were hoping for a simpler, easily understood explanation. However, the very topic, The Meaning of Life, is not an easy topic! How could it be? In fact, it is probably the most difficult topic ever considered.
Now, without further delay,
I can tell you with confidence, that the meaning of life is this;

To believe in Gods Son Jesus Christ, and to grow in the knowledge of Him and of the Father. This world is a schoolhouse, and it prepares those who believe with this knowledge, to live in the Fathers house for all eternity. We are spiritually minded people, we were created that way, quite different than the animals and other forms of creation. Basically, we are the only creation that has an eternal perspective.

This life is not the end. I watched a video the other day with a very well know action celebrity, and a very well-known radio talk show host. They were discussing dying and the celebrity said that death pissed him off! To know that it was going to be all over one day, especially after living a life as good as he has, just didn't seem fair, and pissed him off!
I wanted to reach into the video and shake him until he paid attention and tell him that death of the body is not the end! It is in fact the beginning! If a person does not see that, they are not looking. Sadly, Christianity has been so misrepresented since the time of Jesus. I hear atheists pose their arguments that a loving God cannot exist for one reason or another. One used a tribe of children in Africa that suffered some weird kind of

ailment through no fault of their own. How could a loving God allow this to go on? This is always the question of an atheist when they look at the world and the state of it.

I saw a refrigerator magnet at a friend's house that depicted Jesus standing over the world and using a spiritual eye dropper to randomly give some child alcoholism or drug addiction! This is what many people in the world think about God! They wrongly think that God has created all the ailments and addictions and other bad things that are in the world, and they hate Him for it!

Believers have not represented God, their Father properly at all. They also do not understand the plan which God came up with before the world was even created to give mankind that second chance so to speak because He knew the first chance would be botched by us!

I always want to ask those atheists a question. Do you enjoy your free will? Because in order for mankind to have free will evil has to exist. There is no other way. Yet even when we were bent on self-destruction, God loved us enough to make a way back to Him. That way is in His Son Jesus

Christ. That way is by being born again in spirit with our new spiritual father being none other than God himself! Everything that has happened since the creation of the world, had to happen! The only way to get free will into mankind was to create evil, as well as good. God is not evil, but He had to allow the premise for evil otherwise free will, and along with it, love, could never exist. At least not in the creation. Love was already an attribute of God.

"For God so loved the world, that he sent his only begotten Son, that whosoever shall believe in him, shall have everlasting life."

The trick was to get that same love into mankind without violating them. It seems like a long, roundabout way of getting this done, but for God to be true to Himself, there could be no other way! He had to let mankind fall first, and then, in that fallen state, with free will, man could choose God, or not choose Him. In the beginning, mankind decided to not believe God when God said they would die if they ate the fruit from the tree of knowledge. It was that choice that brought evil into mankind's spirit, which in turn affected his heart. This is why the world is in the state that it is in right now. This is why choosing to believe in Jesus Christ is the single most important decision a person will ever make.

Death of the body is the beginning of a life lived in perfect harmony filled with true peace and joy for those that believe in Jesus Christ, and it will never end.
However, for those who choose not to believe, it is the beginning of an eternity that lacks that perfect harmony, and even worse than that!

Please do not let yourself be a part of the latter group! Now is the time of God's grace. It will not last forever, and even if it lasts another 500 years, as individuals we don't have that long. We are not guaranteed one more minute on this earth!
Sickness, or an accident can take us at any time. How long do you have? Because it ends with either your death, or the return of Jesus for His bride, the church.

You might ask how I know all of this to be the true? To answer that I could talk about how I have searched the scriptures for almost 4 decades. I could list other books and articles I have read over the years, but ultimately, knowing and understanding spiritual truths such as this can only happen by one method! Revelation.

I've lived life away from organized religion. I started out wanting to become a pastor as a young man and decided rather quickly, that wasn't the life for me. I wanted truth. I wanted to know God and for some reason, at least for me, I didn't believe church was going to get me there. The institution of church is fairly good at getting people introduced to the basics. Jesus' death, burial, and resurrection, and helping them come to a decision to believe. However, they lack at helping believers grow up in Christ. The church has become more focused on maintaining their programs and their facilities. Nothing wrong with those things in and of themselves, however if a person wishes to grow up in Christ, to seek Gods mystery, to understand the meaning of life, then I believe the church is failing in that area quite badly!

So, I have lived a life as a self-employed businessman, as a contractor and a business owner. Through all of that, I have searched to know God, to understand what the scriptures mean when they say that Christ comes to live in me if I believe.
I have suffered many things, failed marriages, miscarried children, all the same things that every human deals with in this life. However, the understanding of these truths I have just presented to you have given me hope beyond belief and a reassurance that when this physical life is done, I will step into an eternity filled with all the good things we look for here on this planet. There will be no apprehension, no depression, no hate, nothing evil or deadly will ever again afflict mankind in eternity, as long as it is in Christ. In Christ we will all be family, and love will be the way.

If you are sincere and truth matters to you, God will reveal truth, He will reveal what it means to have Christ in you. Take it from me, since I have come to understand just the little that I know about Gods plan and purpose for us humans, life has been so much more peaceful even in the face of adversity and chaos!

Believe in Jesus Christ today, don't hesitate. No one is guaranteed one more minute on this earth, and the decision must be made before we die.

There is a God
He has a plan
We have a purpose

There is meaning to life!
God Bless!

About the Author:

Scott Halbert, the author of this book, was born in 1963 in Wichita Falls, Texas. Scott grew up in the Pacific Northwest and returned to Texas as a very young man and has been there ever since. Scott has been self-employed most of his life and is a licensed minister of the gospel of Jesus Christ. Though he has had no formal seminary training and has not attended a regular church building in 30 years, his insights into life, as well as the gospel are refreshing and honest and learned through the school of life as taught by the Spirit of God. Scott has been on a journey of truth since he was 21 years old. He is a writer of the Christ Life Message, and you will find his writing to be insightful, and quite possibly different than most anything you have ever read.

If you're not a Christian, please don't let the fact that Scott is a Christian deter you from reading this book. He has a very deep connection to spiritual matters, like few before ever have.

The pursuit of truth, no matter the cost, has always been paramount with Scott. So be assured that everything you read in this book, or any other book written by him has been well thought out and is straight from the heart and he will tell it like he sees it.

Scott's other works are:
The Misrepresentation of God
The Fellowship of The Mystery
The Hidden Gospel

Made in the USA
Middletown, DE
23 September 2022